Christmas Holiday
Willard A. Palmer

Everyone wants to play Christmas music at Christmas time. The teacher who carefully plans the material for each student is likely to find the schedule of progress hopelessly interrupted while the student spends a month or more on Christmas music. The problem is made even more discouraging by the fact that very few piano arrangements of Christmas carols sound like real piano solos or recital pieces, but rather like hymns without texts.

To remedy this situation, Willard A. Palmer has arranged the music in this book so that each selection not only sounds like a piano solo, but emphasizes some important aspect of piano technique. In these solos, the student will have the opportunity to play both homophonic and polyphonic music. The selections include arpeggios with both hands, Alberti basses, a canon imitation, a theme and variations, crossing the hands and other important techniques. Since there are hundreds of elementary carol books available, the selections in this book have been graded at the intermediate level and are placed in the book in approximate order of difficulty.

The entire book may be presented as a pleasing recital program or Christmas concert, with as many students participating as there are selections in the book.

We believe this book contains the perfect answer to the "Christmas interruption" for students at the intermediate level of study.

Contents

Alfred

Revised edition. Copyright © MCMXCIV by Alfred Publishing Co., Inc.
All rights reserved. Printed in USA.
Music engraving: Nancy Butler
Cover photograph: Copyright © 1994 Japack Co./Westlight
Cover design: Ted Engelbart, Laura L. Carlson

In this arrangement the right hand begins the melody and the left hand follows with the same melody one measure behind and five tones lower. This is called a "canon at the fifth below." At letter Ⓐ, the left hand begins and the right hand follows four tones higher. This is called a "canon at the fourth above."

Letter Ⓑ is a contrasting section, with the melody in the right hand. The left hand plays a countermelody. Letter Ⓒ is exactly like the beginning, except both hands play an octave higher on the keyboard. Canons are fun to play. This one resembles, in an elementary way, the type of composition J.S. Bach called a "two-part invention." This will be easier to play if you practice each hand separately at first, then together.

We Wish You a Merry Christmas
(two-part invention)

English Folk Song

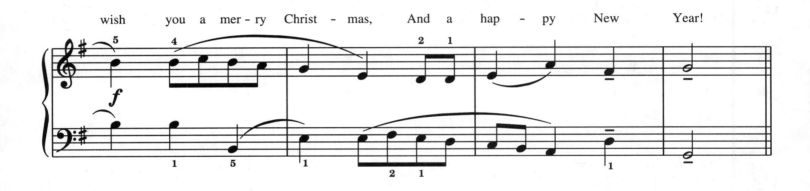

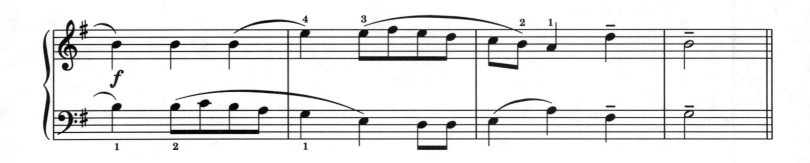

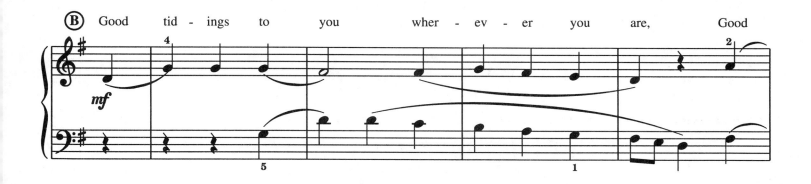

Good tid-ings to you wher-ev-er you are, Good

tid-ings for Christ-mas and a hap-py New Year!

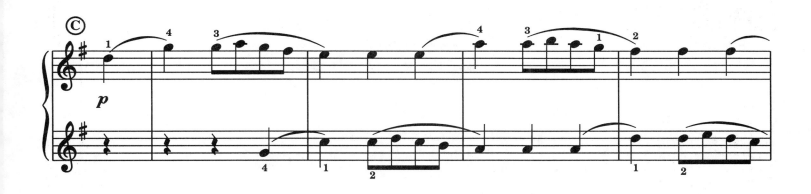

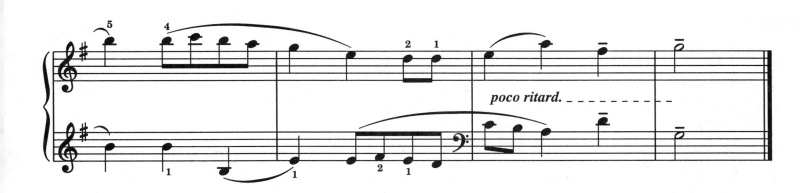

"Bells everywhere . . . filling the air!" There are many different versions of the lyrics to this famous old Ukrainian carol. They are all concerned with the exciting sounds of Christmas bells, which begin softly and gradually grow louder until they seem to be everywhere, then gradually fade away.

Ukrainian Bell Carol

(elementary counterpoint)

M. LEONTOVICH

Brightly

(Optional: Play both hands one octave higher than written throughout.)

*Although the note in the left hand is released on the 3rd count, the pedal sustains the sound of the note throughout the entire measure.

*OSSIA: This Italian word literally means "or maybe." It is used to designate an alternate way of playing a passage. You may play either one of the treble lines. The line just above the bass is a bit more difficult, but it can easily be mastered by practicing the hands separately.

**8va bassa: Play an octave lower.

6

WHAT CHILD IS THIS? is one of the most popular carols. It is based on a very ancient English melody called "Greensleeves." This version uses left-hand arpeggios (broken chords). This style of playing is very effective on the piano, and is also helpful to the student in developing left-hand technique.

What Child Is This?
(left-hand arpeggios)

WILLIAM C. DIX

Old English Air

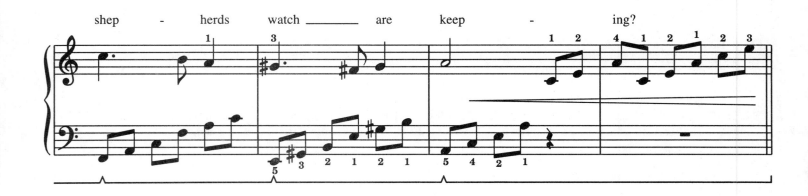

Refrain

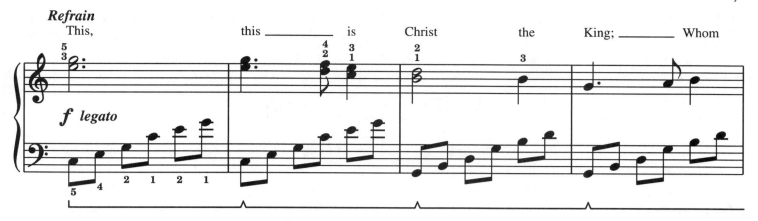

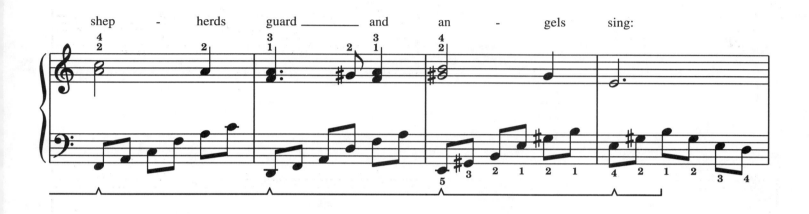

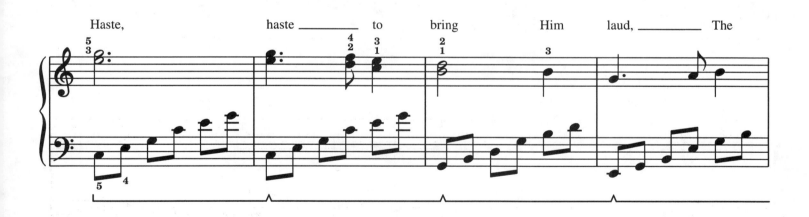

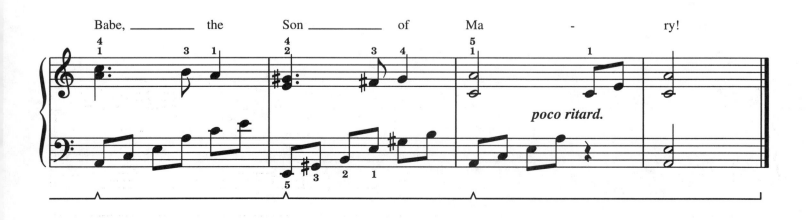

In the first chorus of this arrangement, the right hand plays the melody while the left hand plays broken chord figurations—sometimes called "Alberti bass" (after an eighteenth-century composer who used this style extensively). Another interesting device used in this arrangement is "pedal point." The lowest bass note of each measure in the first chorus is the same, regardless of the changes of harmony. These notes are sustained by the pedal and produce an unusual effect. In the second chorus, the left hand plays the melody while the right hand plays broken chords.

Away in a Manger

(pedal point, Alberti bass, left- and right-hand melody)

MARTIN LUTHER

CARL MUELLER

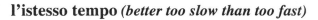

l'istesso tempo *(better too slow than too fast)*

Bring out the left hand melody!

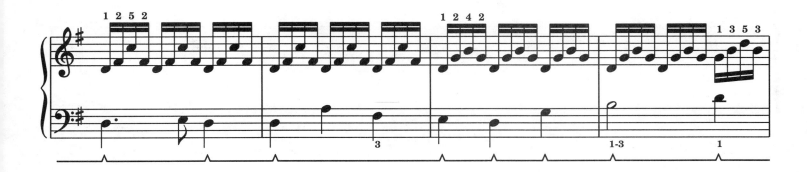

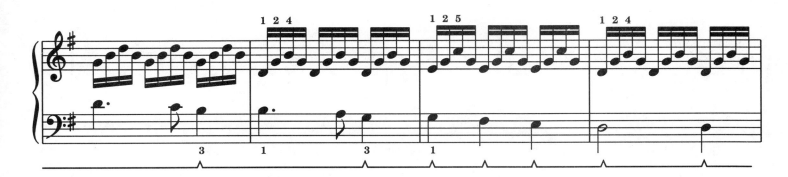

This carol originated in Provence (in southern France) in the 13th century. It was made famous by Georges Bizet who used it in both of the two *L'Arlesienne Suites* in the late nineteenth century.

This version begins with the two hands playing the melody one octave apart. In the eighth measure a canon begins, with the left hand following the right hand one octave lower. This is called a "canon at the octave below." After a contrasting section, the canon resumes. "Alla marcia" means "like a march." Play this with a steady, even tempo.

March of the Three Kings

(with a canon at the octave)

Provençal Melody

Alla marcia

"Silent Night" sounds particularly beautiful when it is sung by two choirs, one on the stage and one offstage. The second choir echoes the sound of the first choir. A similar effect can be produced on the piano by playing the echoed phrases softly, and in a different octave. The right hand plays the notes with stems pointing up and the left hand plays those with the stems pointing down.

Silent Night
(with echo effects)

JOSEPH MÖHR   FRANZ GRÜBER

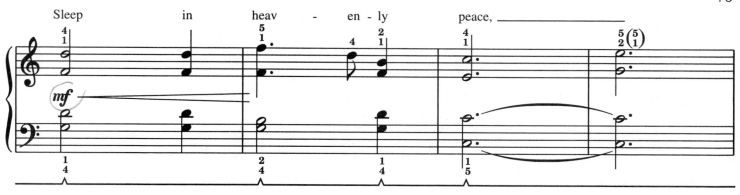

Sleep in heav - en - ly peace, _____

Sleep _____ in heav - en - ly peace. _____

Here is another way to play "Silent Night."

The right hand plays the melody in the upper part of the bass staff, so it sounds like a male voice. The left hand plays bass and two-note chords. The bass is played on the first count of each measure, below the melody. The left hand then crosses over the right hand to play the chords on the second and third counts. In this version, the right hand plays all the notes with stems pointing up and the left hand plays all the notes with stems pointing down. You may add this version to the previous one, to make a longer arrangement of "Silent Night."

Silent Night

(crossing the left hand over the right hand)

(Pedal optional)

pedal simile

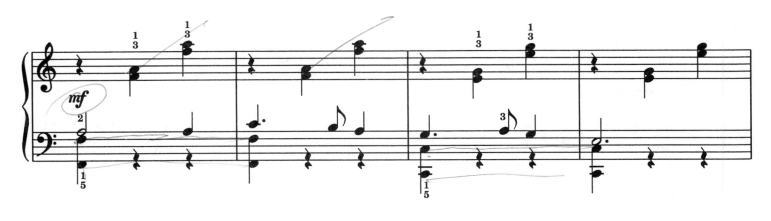

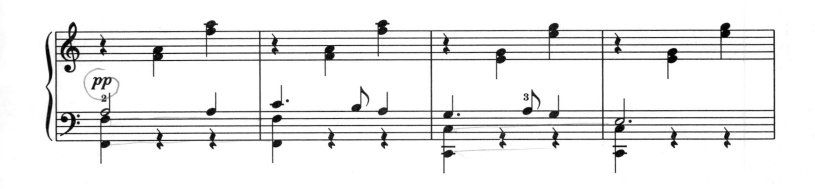

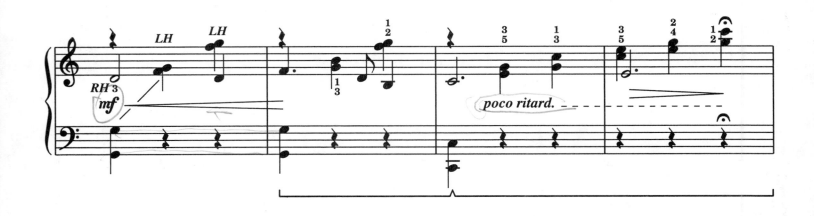

Less motion

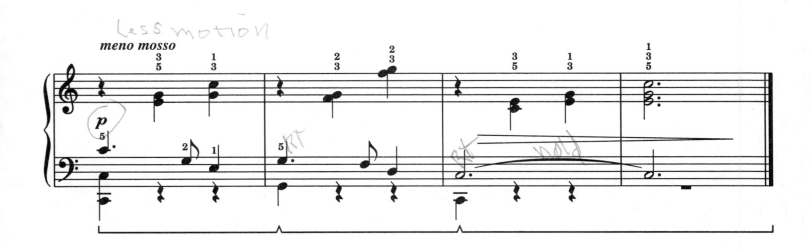

In this version of "Jingle Bells," the right hand imitates the sound of sleigh bells by playing two neighboring notes on the keyboard at the same time. The left hand plays a bass note on the first count of each measure and holds it for the entire measure, while staccato chords are played on the "ands" of the measure.

¢, or Alla Breve time, is correctly counted "one-and-two-and." A half note gets one count.

Jingle Bells
(with sleigh bell imitations)

J. PIERPONT

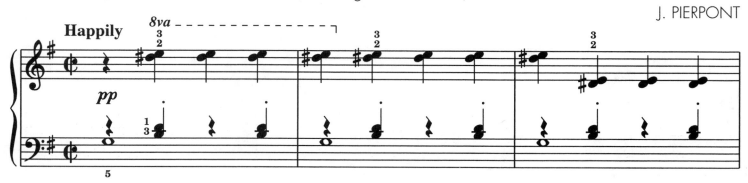

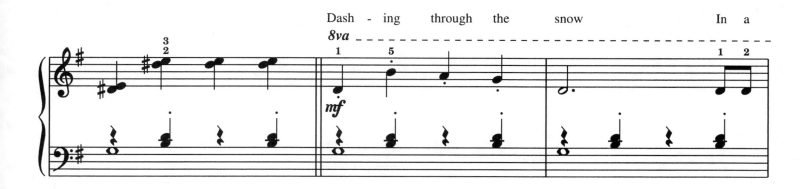

Dash - ing through the snow In a

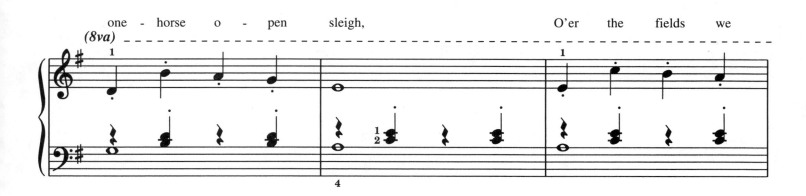

one - horse o - pen sleigh, O'er the fields we

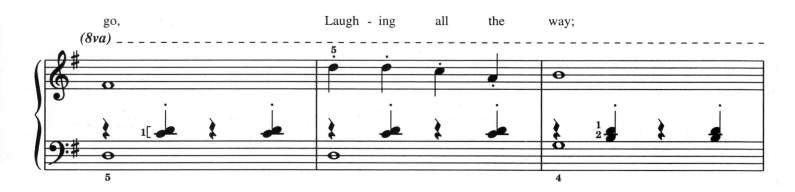

go, Laugh - ing all the way;

16

This is one of the greatest of all Christmas carols. We should not be surprised to learn that it was written by the famous George Frideric Handel, who wrote the wonderful oratorio, the *Messiah*. The second chorus is a departure from the usual way of playing this. It begins with the melody in octaves in the left hand. The right hand plays a florid countermelody somewhat in Handel's own style. This is an excellent octave study for the left hand.

Joy to the World
(left-hand octave study)

ISAAC WATTS

G.F. HANDEL

*At this point, many versions add an extra measure to preserve the four-measure phrases to which our ears are accustomed. Handel deliberately omitted a measure here to make the song seem to plunge ahead, giving it a feeling of great enthusiasm and joy.

The romantic quality of this beautiful carol is heightened by the use of arpeggiated chords. The word "arpeggiated" means "played in the manner of a harp." The wavy line to the left of the chords indicates that the chord is broken by playing the lower note first, then quickly adding the higher notes one at a time in rapid succession. After each note is played, it is held so that, finally, all the notes are heard together. When the wavy line includes the notes of the left and right hands, the notes of the left hand are played first followed by the notes of the right hand, to make a continuous broken chord without hesitation between the two hands.

Sleep, Holy Babe

(arpeggiated chords)

EDWARD CASWELL

J.B. DYKES

"The Twelve Days of Christmas" is called a "cumulative song," because each verse adds a new phrase and the song becomes longer and longer. If you do not wish this solo to be so long, you may simply play it straight through without any repeats and take the final ending the first time. This arrangement contains many interesting countermelodies, and if you listen carefully you can actually hear the "five gold rings," the "lords a-leaping," the "drummers drumming," the "ladies dancing," etc.

The Twelve Days of Christmas

(study in counterpoint)

Old English Carol

Moderately fast

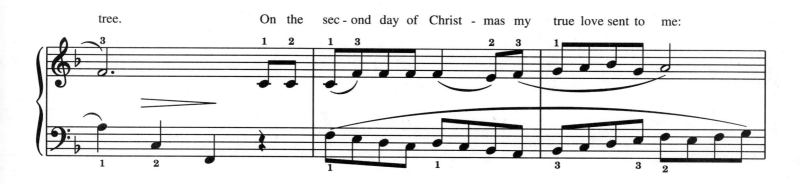

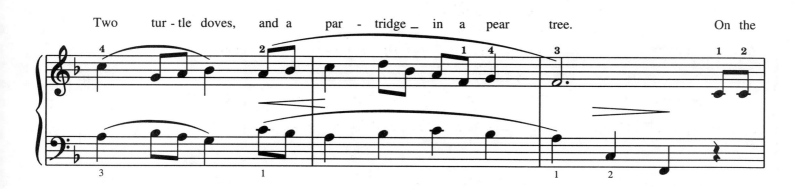

22

24

In a theme and variations the melody is played first in a simple, unadorned style. This is called the "statement of the theme." The variations closely follow the melody or harmony (or both) of the theme but add variety and contrast by the use of different rhythms, tempos, etc. This form of music never fails to please audiences. Proceed to each of the variations from the previous movement without interruption.

Coventry Carol
(theme and variations)

ROBERT CROO

Old English Melody

THEME

VAR. I

Moderately slow

VAR. II*

Marche funebre

---

* FUNERAL MARCH: An appropriate variation, because the third verse of the carol is concerned with Herod's slaying of all the new-born male children.

VAR. III*
Moderato

do fingering

* Note the similarity between the notes used in Var. III and those of the theme.

** Play both hands very staccato, so that the F's don't collide with one another.

VAR. IV*
Moderato

OPTIONAL:
Repeat Var. III
with both hands 8va

p   simile   ritard.

* Note the similarity between the notes of Var. IV and those of the theme.

Instrumental music that tells a story, depicts a scene, or calls forth certain mental images is called "program" music. This is the opposite of "absolute" or "abstract" music, which exists only for the sake of its own sound and is not descriptive at all. "Parade of the Tin Soldiers" is program music because it paints the picture the title suggests. At the end, we actually hear the soldiers falling down. Although this is not a carol, it is considered very appropriate for the Christmas season and is often heard during the holidays.

Parade of the Tin Soldiers

(descriptive program music)

LEON JESSEL

*An optional cut may be made, omitting the measures between Ⓐ and Ⓑ.

32

* Last note of glissando may be played with the LEFT HAND.